THE SLIM 800 HOT AIR FRYER
The Essential High Protein Cookbook

THE SLIM 800 HOT AIR FRYER ESSENTIAL HIGH PROTEIN COOKBOOK

978-1-913005-51-1

DISCLAIMER

Except for use in any review, the reproduction or utilisation of this work in whole or in part in any form by any electronic, mechanical or other means, now known or hereafter invented, including xerography, photocopying and recording, or in any information storage or retrieval system, is forbidden without the permission of the publisher.

This book is sold subject to the condition that it shall not, by way of trade or otherwise, be lent, resold, hired out or otherwise circulated without the prior consent of the publisher in any form of binding or cover other than that in which it is published and without a similar condition including this condition being imposed on the subsequent purchaser.

This book is designed to provide information on meals & snacks that can be made using an electric hot air fryer appliance. Some recipes may contain nuts or traces of nuts. Those suffering from any allergies associated with nuts should avoid any recipes containing nuts or nut based oils. This information is provided and sold with the knowledge that the publisher and author do not offer any legal or other professional advice. In the case of a need for any such expertise consult with the appropriate professional.

This book does not contain all information available on the subject, and other sources of recipes are available.
Every effort has been made to make this book as accurate as possible. However, there may be typographical and or content errors. Therefore, this book should serve only as a general guide and not as the ultimate source of subject information.

This book contains information that might be dated and is intended only to educate and entertain.
The author and publisher shall have no liability or responsibility to any person or entity regarding any loss or damage incurred, or alleged to have incurred, directly or indirectly, by the information contained in this book.

CONTENTS

INTRODUCTION	8

POULTRY — 11

Pesto Chicken & Green Beans	12
Turkey & Quinoa Bake	13
Herbed Turkey & Roasted Broccoli	14
Maple Glazed Chicken & Brussels Sprouts	15
High-Protein Turkey Meatball Salad	16
Garlic Herb Chicken & Asparagus	17
Lime Chicken & Black Bean Bowl	18
Sesame Ginger Chicken Stir-Fry	19
BBQ Chicken & Corn Bake	20
Coconut Lime Chicken Thighs	21
Greek Chicken & Spinach Wrap	22
Sriracha Honey Chicken & Peppers	23
Balsamic Chicken & Brussels Sprouts	24
Cajun Chicken & Rice	25
Roasted Chicken with Sweet Potatoes	26

MEAT — 27

Honey-Balsamic Pork	28
Mustard-Crusted Pork Chops	29
Herbed Lamb Steaks	30
Peppered Steaks with Green Beans	31
Stuffed Pork Tenderloin	32
Rosemary Lamb Skewers	33
Spiced Beef & Sweet Potato Hash	34
BBQ Ribs with Coleslaw	35
Spicy Beef & Bean Chili	36

Savory Beef with Sweet Berries — 37
Garlic Soy Beef, Rice & Greens — 38

FISH — 39

Tuna & Sweet Potato Bowls — 40
Garlic Prawn & Veggie Medley — 41
Lemon Cod with Baby Potatoes — 42
Crispy Sesame Tuna with Broccoli — 43
Prawn & Asparagus Frittata — 44
Prawn & Cauliflower Rice Bowls — 45
Spicy Prawns with Quinoa — 46

VEGGIES — 47

Parmesan Aubergine with Fresh Tomatoes — 48
Stuffed Mushrooms — 49
Halloumi & Veg Skewers — 50
Tofu Stir-Fry with Peanut Sauce — 51
Cauliflower Steaks with Tzatziki — 52
Stuffed Pine Nut Courgettes — 53
Squash with Goat Cheese — 54
Sweet Potato & Black Bean Tacos — 55
Tahini Cauliflower Bowl — 56
Aubergine Lentil Salad — 57
Paprika Brussels Sprouts — 58
Courgette & Lentil Yoghurt Fritters — 59
Spinach & Peppers with Cottage Cheese — 60
Edamame Stir-Fry — 61
Edamame & Rice Balls — 62

EGGS, EGGS, EGGS — 63

Spinach & Feta Egg Cups — 64
Cheesy Egg-Stuffed Pepper — 65
Mushroom & Ham Omelette — 66
Baked Avocado Egg — 67
Egg & Chicken Sausage Scramble — 68

Egg & Quinoa Breakfast Bowl	69
Egg-Stuffed Portobello Mushrooms	70
Egg & Salmon Avocado Toast	71
Egg & Turkey Rashers	72
Courgette & Egg Frittata	73
Eggs in Purgatory	74
Smoked Salmon & Egg Bowl	75
Eggs & Cheddar Toast	76
Mediterranean Egg Cups	77
Mushroom & Egg Breakfast Skillet	78
Spinach & Egg Stuffed Tomatoes	79
Egg-Stuffed Sweet Potato	80
Egg & Veggie Hash	81
Herbed Egg White Bites	82
Turkish Eggs	83
Honey Feta Eggs	84

PROTEIN SNACKS — 85

Crispy Chickpea Snacks / Edamame Bites	86
Tofu Cubes with Soy Sauce / Lentil Falafel Balls	87
Roasted Almonds with Spices / Halloumi Fingers	88
Peanut Butter Stuffed Dates / Crispy Broad Beans	89
Parmesan Courgette Chips / Black Bean Quesadilla Slices	90
Spiced Cashew Mix / Tempeh Cubes with Soy Glaze	91
Kale Chips / Cauliflower Bites with Almond Crust	92
Sweet Potato & Lentil Balls / Spicy Pumpkin Seeds	93
Pea Fritters / Paprika Butter Beans	94
Roasted Carrot & Quinoa Bites / Almond Butter Apple Slices	95

INTRODUCTION

What Is the Slim '800' Lifestyle?

The Slim 800 Diet is an effort to return to a healthier way of eating that emphasises fasting and balanced nutrition. Fasting is probably most well-known as the 5:2 Diet—a great and flexible way to approach weight loss and less restrictive than many other diets. The 5:2 approach means you can eat 'normally' for 5 days a week and fast for 2. It's revolutionized the way people think about dieting.

By allowing you the freedom to eat normally for MOST of the week and fast by restricting your calorie intake for just TWO non-consecutive days a week (800 calories per day for men and women), you keep yourself motivated and remove that dreaded feeling of constantly denying yourself the food you really want to eat. It still takes willpower, but it's nowhere near as much of a grind when you know that you have tomorrow to look forward to. It's all about freedom. The ability to be flexible with the days you choose to fast makes the likelihood of you sticking to the diet for a prolonged period, or even indefinitely as a lifestyle choice, much higher than a regime that requires calorie restriction every single day.

Protein plays a crucial role in this approach, as it helps maintain muscle mass, boosts metabolism, and keeps you feeling fuller for longer, making it easier to stick to your fasting days without feeling deprived.

With The Slim 800: Hot Air Fryer - The Essential High Protein Cookbook, we've given you lots of air fryer recipe ideas that are high in protein and can be used on your fast days and on your 'normal' days. Everything is calorie counted with nutritional breakdowns, so you'll be able to keep things on track more easily while enjoying delicious, protein-packed meals.

Your ultimate guide to high-protein, healthier frying.

Hot air fryers are revolutionising the way we cook, becoming an indispensable addition to the modern kitchen. Once you experience the convenience and health benefits of a hot air fryer, you'll wonder how you ever lived without one!

A hot air fryer allows you to create quick, easy, and healthy meals with just a fraction of the oil required by traditional frying methods. There's no need for preheating and it can cook a wide variety of dishes, from snacks to main courses—not just chips! Speaking of which, air-fried chips deserve a special mention for their crispy perfection achieved with minimal oil, making them a healthier option.

The Slim 800: Hot Air Fryer - The Essential High Protein Cookbook is your ultimate guide to high-protein, healthier frying. It features a diverse collection of recipes, including starters, main courses, sides, and even desserts, all with a focus on boosting your protein intake. Whether you're preparing a family meal, hosting a party or indulging in a snack, this cookbook has you covered. It's the only hot air fryer recipe book you'll ever need!

Simple, Quick, Convenient, High-Protein, and Nutritious

This book is designed for those who value simplicity and convenience without sacrificing nutrition. A high-protein diet supports muscle growth, aids weight management, and provides sustained energy throughout the day. Whether you're on a busy schedule or just looking to make healthier choices, the recipes in this book are crafted to be quick, easy, and rich in protein—perfect for anyone who wants to eat well without spending hours in the kitchen.

> *We use fresh, inexpensive, lower-calorie and lower-fat ingredients, all readily available at your local supermarket.*

HOW DOES HOT AIR FRYING WORK?

Unlike traditional deep frying, a hot air fryer uses very hot air (up to 200°C) to circulate around the food, cooking it quickly with a crispy outer layer.

TEMPERATURE CONTROL

Most air fryers come with adjustable temperature controls and timers. If yours doesn't, it's likely preset to cook at 200°C/400°F. Keep an eye on cooking times to ensure perfect results.

HOW CAN IT FRY WITH SO LITTLE OIL?

The efficient hot air circulation requires only a minimal amount of oil. Often, a light spray of oil is enough, making it the healthiest way to fry. Choose your preferred low-calorie spray oil, whether it's olive, coconut, or sunflower oil.

DOES HOT AIR FRIED FRIED FOOD TASTE DIFFERENT?

Hot air fried food often tastes better than traditional fried food. The reduced-fat content doesn't compromise flavour, and the method preserves the natural taste of your ingredients.

CLEANER, SAFER, HEALTHIER

Hot air fryers use significantly less oil—often just a spoonful—making them a healthier option compared to traditional deep fryers. They use fresh oil for each cooking session, eliminating strong odours and smoke. This method is not only healthier but also safer, with most fryers pausing the cooking process when the lid is lifted.

OUR RECIPES

Reflecting the simplicity of hot air frying, our recipes are easy to follow with minimal preparation and cooking times. We use fresh, inexpensive, lower-calorie and lower-fat ingredients, all readily available at your local supermarket. Each recipe includes calorie counts and nutritional information, perfect for those following an 800-calorie fasting day. We minimise the use of store cupboard ingredients to keep your store cupboard streamlined and your cooking affordable. Some recipes serve four, and given that air fryer capacities vary, you might need to adjust cooking times for batch cooking.

TIPS

To get the best results from your hot air fryer, keep these tips in mind:

- Remove food promptly once cooking is complete to maintain crispiness.
- Clean your appliance after each use; most parts are dishwasher safe.
- Avoid abrasive cleaning materials to protect the non-stick coating.
- Ensure food has plenty of space in the fryer for even cooking.
- Read the manufacturer's instructions thoroughly to understand your fryer's functions and maintain the warranty.
- Air fryers vary in capacity; you may need to cook in batches.
- Preheat your air fryer before adding food.
- Cooking times are guidelines; check your food to ensure it's thoroughly cooked before serving.

♥ POULTRY

PESTO CHICKEN & GREEN BEANS

Serves 4

INGREDIENTS

- 4 skinless chicken breasts
- 300g green beans, trimmed
- 2 tbsp reduced-fat pesto sauce
- 1 tsp garlic powder
- 1 tsp dried oregano
- 1 tbsp grated Parmesan cheese
- Low-calorie spray oil
- Salt & pepper to season
- Lemon wedges for serving

METHOD

1 Spray the green beans with oil. Season and sprinkle with garlic powder. Add to the air fryer basket and cook at 180°C (350°F) for 7 minutes.

2 While the green beans are cooking, season the chicken breasts, spray with oil, and combine with pesto sauce, oregano, salt, and pepper.

3 Add the chicken to the air fryer basket and cook at 180°C (350°F) for an additional 15-18 minutes, or until the chicken is cooked through.

4 In the last 3 minutes of cooking, sprinkle the Parmesan cheese over the chicken and green beans. Continue cooking until the cheese is melted and slightly crispy. Serve with lemon wedges on the side.

NUTRITION

- Protein: 35g
- Calories: 310 kcal
- Total Fat: 14g
- Saturated Fat: 4g
- Carbohydrates: 5g
- Fibre: 2g
- Sugars: 2g

TURKEY & QUINOA BAKE

Serves 4

INGREDIENTS

- 1 onion, finely chopped
- 2 garlic cloves, crushed
- 1 courgette, chopped
- 1 red pepper, chopped
- 100g pitted olives, halved
- 250g leftover cooked turkey, shredded
- 500g pre-cooked quinoa
- 2 eggs, beaten
- 1 tbsp each tomato puree, dried oregano, basil & smoked paprika
- 1 lemon, juiced and zested
- 30g reduced-fat goat cheese, crumbled
- Low-calorie spray oil
- Salt & pepper to season

NUTRITION

- Protein: 24g
- Calories: 330 kcal
- Total Fat: 11g
- Saturated Fat: 3g
- Carbohydrates: 30g
- Fibre: 6g
- Sugars: 4g

METHOD

1 In a large bowl, combine the chopped onion, garlic, courgette, and pepper. Season with salt, pepper, oregano, basil and smoked paprika. Spray with low-calorie oil.

2 Place the mixture in an air fryer-safe dish and cook at 180°C (350°F) for 8-10 minutes, stirring halfway through, until the vegetables are softened. Add the shredded turkey, pre-cooked quinoa, tomato puree, lemon zest, lemon juice, and beaten eggs to the dish. Stir to combine everything evenly.

3 Return the dish to the air fryer and cook for an additional 7-9 minutes at 180°C (350°F), stirring occasionally to ensure even cooking and that the eggs are fully set.

4 Once the bake is cooked through, remove from the air fryer and stir in the olives. Sprinkle with goat cheese on top and serve.

HERBED TURKEY & ROASTED BROCCOLI

Serves 4

INGREDIENTS

- 4 small turkey fillets
- 200g tender-stem broccoli
- 1 tsp garlic powder
- 2 tbsp olive oil
- 1 tsp dried rosemary
- 1 tsp dried thyme
- 1 lemon (zest and juice)
- Salt & pepper to season
- 2 tbsp freshly chopped chives

NUTRITION

- Protein: 34g
- Calories: 295 kcal
- Total Fat: 14g
- Saturated Fat: 3g
- Carbohydrates: 6g
- Fibre: 3g
- Sugars: 2g

METHOD

1 In a large bowl, combine the broccoli with the garlic, 1 tbsp olive oil, salt, and pepper. Add to the air fryer basket and cook at 180°C (350°F) for 10 minutes.

2 While the broccoli is cooking, season the turkey fillets with rosemary, thyme, lemon zest, and the remaining olive oil.

3 After the broccoli has cooked for 10 minutes, add the seasoned turkey fillets to the air fryer basket. Continue cooking for an additional 14-18 minutes, or until the turkey is cooked through and piping hot.

4 Drizzle with fresh lemon juice, sprinkle with chopped chives, and serve.

MAPLE GLAZED CHICKEN & BRUSSELS SPROUTS

Serves 4

INGREDIENTS

- 2 onions, sliced
- 300g Brussels sprouts, halved
- 2 tsp garlic powder
- 4 small chicken fillets
- ½ tsp each of salt, cumin & smoked paprika
- 2 tbsp maple syrup
- 1 tbsp balsamic vinegar
- 2 tbsp freshly chopped thyme
- Low-calorie spray oil
- Salt & pepper to season

NUTRITION

- Protein: 29g
- Calories: 320 kcal
- Total Fat: 8g
- Saturated Fat: 2g
- Carbohydrates: 26g
- Fibre: 4g
- Sugars: 12g

METHOD

1 Place the onions, Brussels sprouts and garlic powder in a large bowl. Spray with oil, season and combine. Add to the air fryer basket and cook at 180°C (350°F) for 10 minutes.

2 While the vegetables are cooking, season the chicken fillets with salt, cumin and smoked paprika. Lightly spray with oil. After the vegetables have cooked for 10 minutes, add the seasoned chicken fillets to the air fryer basket.

3 In a small bowl, mix the maple syrup with balsamic vinegar and drizzle over the chicken and Brussels sprouts. Cook for an additional 18-22 minutes at 180°C (350°F) or until the chicken is cooked through and piping hot.

4 Sprinkle with thyme and serve.

HIGH-PROTEIN TURKEY MEATBALL SALAD

Serves 4

INGREDIENTS

- 500g turkey mince
- 2 garlic cloves, crushed
- 2 tbsp oat flour
- 1 tsp Italian seasoning
- 200g mixed greens
- 125g cherry tomatoes, halved
- 100g cucumber, sliced
- 2 tbsp balsamic vinaigrette
- 30g low-fat feta cheese, crumbled
- Salt & pepper to season

NUTRITION

- Protein: 31g
- Calories: 350 kcal
- Total Fat: 17g
- Saturated Fat: 4g
- Carbohydrates: 10g
- Fibre: 3g
- Sugars: 4g

METHOD

1 Combine turkey mince, garlic, oat flour, and Italian seasoning. Form into 16-20 small meatballs.

2 Air fry the meatballs at 180°C (350°F) for 12-15 minutes or until cooked through.

3 Toss the mixed greens, cherry tomatoes, cucumber, and vinaigrette in a large bowl.

4 Top the salad with cooked meatballs and crumbled feta cheese. Season and serve.

GARLIC HERB CHICKEN & ASPARAGUS

Serves 4

INGREDIENTS

- 500g chicken breast, sliced
- 200g asparagus
- 1 tsp garlic powder
- 1 tsp dried thyme
- 1 tbsp olive oil
- 30g grated Parmesan cheese
- Salt & pepper to season
- Lemon wedges for serving

NUTRITION

- Protein: 36g
- Calories: 320 kcal
- Total Fat: 13g
- Saturated Fat: 3g
- Carbohydrates: 8g
- Fibre: 3g
- Sugars: 2g

METHOD

1 Toss the chicken slices with garlic powder, thyme and olive oil. Add the asparagus and mix well.

2 Place in the air fryer basket and cook at 180°C (350°F) for 12-14 minutes, shaking halfway through.

3 Sprinkle with Parmesan cheese in the last 2 minutes of cooking.

4 Season and serve with lemon wedges.

LIME CHICKEN & BLACK BEAN BOWL

Serves 4

INGREDIENTS

- 500g chicken breast, cubed
- 1 tin (400g) black beans, drained and rinsed
- 1 red onion, chopped
- 1 red pepper, chopped
- 1 tsp cumin
- 1 tsp chili powder
- 2 tbsp lime juice
- 1 tbsp olive oil
- 2 tbsp fresh coriander, chopped
- Low-calorie spray oil
- Salt & pepper to season

METHOD

1 Toss the chicken, black beans, onion, and pepper with cumin, chili powder, lime juice and olive oil.

2 Place the mixture in the air fryer and cook at 180°C (350°F) for 14-16 minutes, shaking halfway through.

3 Garnish with fresh coriander. Season and serve.

NUTRITION

- Protein: 32g
- Calories: 340 kcal
- Total Fat: 9g
- Saturated Fat: 2g
- Carbohydrates: 28g
- Fibre: 9g
- Sugars: 3g

SESAME GINGER CHICKEN STIR-FRY

Serves 4

INGREDIENTS

- 800g chicken breast, sliced
- 200g sugar snap peas
- 1 red pepper, sliced
- 2 tbsp soy sauce
- 2 tbsp sesame oil
- 1 tsp grated ginger
- 2 garlic cloves, crushed
- 1 tbsp sesame seeds
- 1 bunch spring onions, chopped

METHOD

1 Combine chicken slices, peas, peppers, soy sauce, sesame oil, ginger, and garlic in a bowl.

2 Place in the air fryer and cook at 180°C (350°F) for 12-14 minutes, shaking halfway through.

3 Garnish with sesame seeds and green onions before serving.

NUTRITION

- Protein: 34g
- Calories: 340 kcal
- Total Fat: 15g
- Saturated Fat: 2g
- Carbohydrates: 10g
- Fibre: 3g
- Sugars: 4g

BBQ CHICKEN & CORN BAKE

Serves 4

INGREDIENTS

- 800g chicken breast, cubed
- 200g frozen sweetcorn
- 1 red onion, sliced
- 1 red pepper, sliced
- 2 tbsp BBQ sauce
- 1 tsp smoked paprika
- Low-calorie spray oil
- Salt & pepper to season

NUTRITION

- Protein: 35g
- Calories: 370 kcal
- Total Fat: 12g
- Saturated Fat: 3g
- Carbohydrates: 28g
- Fibre: 5g
- Sugars: 9g

METHOD

1 Toss chicken, corn, onion, and bell pepper with BBQ sauce, smoked paprika, salt, and pepper.

2 Place in the air fryer basket and cook at 180°C (350°F) for 14-16 minutes, shaking halfway through.

3 Season and serve.

COCONUT LIME CHICKEN THIGHS

Serves 4

INGREDIENTS

- 2 tsp garlic powder
- 2 tsp ground cumin
- 2 tbsp desiccated coconut
- 1 lime, juiced and zested
- 1 tbsp olive oil
- 1 red onion, sliced
- 200g cherry tomatoes, halved
- Salt & pepper to season

NUTRITION

- Protein: 32g
- Calories: 360 kcal
- Total Fat: 16g
- Saturated Fat: 5g
- Carbohydrates: 9g
- Fibre: 3g
- Sugars: 4g

METHOD

1 Toss chicken thighs with garlic powder, cumin, desiccated coconut, lime juice, lime zest, and olive oil. Add onion and cherry tomatoes, and mix well.

2 Place in the air fryer and cook at 180°C (350°F) for 15-18 minutes until the chicken is cooked through.

3 Season and serve.

GREEK CHICKEN & SPINACH WRAP

Serves 4

INGREDIENTS

- 500g chicken breast, cubed
- 1 tsp dried oregano
- 2 garlic cloves, minced
- 1 lemon, juiced and zested
- 150g spinach leaves
- 100g reduced-fat feta cheese, crumbled
- 4 large whole grain wraps
- Salt & pepper to season

NUTRITION

- Protein: 30g
- Calories: 340 kcal
- Total Fat: 11g
- Saturated Fat: 4g
- Carbohydrates: 32g
- Fibre: 5g
- Sugars: 3g

METHOD

1 Toss the chicken with oregano, garlic, lemon juice, lemon zest, salt and pepper.

2 Cook in the air fryer at 180°C (350°F) for 12-14 minutes until cooked through.

3 In the last 2 minutes, add spinach leaves to wilt slightly.

4 Serve in whole-grain wraps with crumbled feta on top.

SRIRACHA HONEY CHICKEN & PEPPERS

Serves 4

INGREDIENTS

- 800g chicken breast, sliced
- 1 red pepper, sliced
- 1 yellow pepper, sliced
- 1 red onion, sliced
- 2 tbsp sriracha sauce
- 1 tbsp honey
- 1 tsp garlic powder
- 1 tbsp olive oil
- 100g salad laves
- Salt & pepper to season

METHOD

1 Toss chicken with sriracha, honey, garlic powder, olive oil, salt, and pepper. Add sliced peppers and onion.

2 Place in the air fryer and cook at 180°C (350°F) for 12-14 minutes, shaking halfway through.

3 Season and serve with salad leaves.

NUTRITION

- Protein: 31g
- Calories: 310 kcal
- Total Fat: 9g
- Saturated Fat: 2g
- Carbohydrates: 25g
- Fibre: 6g
- Sugars: 12g

BALSAMIC CHICKEN & BRUSSELS SPROUTS

Serves 4

INGREDIENTS

- 500g chicken breast, cubed
- 300g Brussels sprouts, halved
- 1 red onion, sliced
- 2 tbsp balsamic vinegar
- 1 tsp Dijon mustard
- 1 tbsp olive oil
- 1 tsp garlic powder
- Salt & pepper to season
- 4 large beef tomatoes, sliced

METHOD

1 Toss chicken, Brussels sprouts, and onion with balsamic vinegar, Dijon mustard, garlic powder, olive oil, salt and pepper.

2 Place in the air fryer and cook at 180°C (350°F) for 14-16 minutes, shaking halfway through.

3 Serve hot alongside sliced tomatoes seasoned with lots of black pepper.

NUTRITION

- Protein: 33g
- Calories: 320 kcal
- Total Fat: 10g
- Saturated Fat: 2g
- Carbohydrates: 24g
- Fibre: 7g
- Sugars: 8g

CAJUN CHICKEN & RICE

Serves 4

INGREDIENTS

- 1 onion, chopped
- 2 garlic cloves, crushed
- 1 red pepper, chopped
- 250g chicken breast, cubed
- 500g pre-cooked wild rice
- 2 eggs, beaten
- 1 tbsp Cajun seasoning
- 1 tsp smoked paprika
- 1 tbsp tomato paste
- 30g reduced-fat cheddar cheese, grated
- Low-calorie spray oil
- Salt & pepper to season

NUTRITION

- Protein: 30g
- Calories: 340 kcal
- Total Fat: 10g
- Saturated Fat: 3g
- Carbohydrates: 32g
- Fibre: 4g
- Sugars: 3g

METHOD

1 Season the cubed chicken breast with salt, pepper, and a little Cajun seasoning. Spray with oil and place in the air fryer basket. Cook at 180°C (350°F) for 8-10 minutes, shaking halfway through, until the chicken is fully cooked. Remove and set aside.

2 In a large bowl, combine the chopped onion, garlic, and red pepper with the remaining Cajun seasoning and smoked paprika. Spray with low-calorie spray oil and toss to coat. Place the vegetable mixture in an air fryer safe dish and cook at 180°C (350°F) for 8-10 minutes, stirring halfway through, until the vegetables are softened.

3 Add the cooked chicken, pre-cooked wild rice, tomato paste, and beaten eggs to the air-fried vegetables. Mix well to combine all ingredients.

4 Cook for an additional 7-9 minutes, stirring occasionally, until the eggs are fully set and the dish is heated through. Sprinkle the grated reduced-fat cheddar cheese over the top and cook for an additional 2-3 minutes until the cheese is melted. Season and serve.

ROASTED CHICKEN WITH SWEET POTATOES

Serves 4

INGREDIENTS

- 500g chicken breast, sliced into strips
- 200g green beans, trimmed
- 2 medium sweet potatoes, cubed
- 1 tsp garlic powder
- 1 tsp lemon pepper seasoning
- 2 tbsp olive oil
- 1 lemon, zest & juice
- Salt & pepper to season
- 2 tbsp freshly chopped flat leaf parsley

NUTRITION

- Protein: 38g
- Calories: 410 kcal
- Total Fat: 12g
- Saturated Fat: 2g
- Carbohydrates: 30g
- Fibre: 6g
- Sugars: 7g

METHOD

1 Toss the sweet potato cubes with 1 tbsp of olive oil, salt and pepper. Place the sweet potatoes in the air fryer basket and cook at 180°C (350°F) for 10 minutes.

2 While the sweet potatoes are cooking, toss the chicken strips with garlic powder, lemon pepper seasoning, the remaining olive oil and lemon zest. Add the green beans and mix well.

3 After 10 minutes, add the chicken and green beans to the air fryer basket with the sweet potatoes. Cook for an additional 12-15 minutes, shaking halfway through, until the chicken is cooked through, the green beans are tender, and the sweet potatoes are golden brown.

4 Drizzle with fresh lemon juice, sprinkle with chopped parsley, season and serve.

♥
MEAT

HONEY-BALSAMIC PORK

Serves 4

INGREDIENTS

- 4 pork tenderloin medallions (about 200g each)
- 2 tbsp balsamic vinegar
- 2 tbsp honey
- 1 tsp dried oregano
- 1 tsp garlic powder
- 1 red onion, sliced
- 1 yellow pepper, sliced
- 200g asparagus
- 250g pre-cooked quinoa
- Low-calorie spray oil
- Salt & pepper to season

NUTRITION

- Protein: 38g
- Calories: 400
- Total Fat: 10g
- Saturated Fat: 3g
- Carbohydrates: 30g
- Fibre: 5g
- Sugars: 8g

METHOD

1 In a bowl, whisk together balsamic vinegar, honey, oregano and garlic powder. Season with salt and pepper.

2 Toss the red onion, pepper, and asparagus with low-calorie spray oil and season. Cook in the air fryer at 180°C (350°F) for 5 minutes.

3 Push vegetables to the sides and place pork medallions in the centre. Brush with the honey-balsamic glaze. Cook for 5-7 minutes, flip, brush with more glaze, and cook for another 5-7 minutes until cooked through.

4 Serve the pork medallions on a bed of quinoa with the roasted vegetables on the side.

MUSTARD-CRUSTED PORK CHOPS

Serves 4

INGREDIENTS

- 4 bone-in pork chops (about 180g each)
- 2 tbsp Dijon mustard
- 1 tsp dried thyme
- 1 tsp garlic powder
- 400g sweet potatoes, cut into wedges
- 1 red onion, sliced
- 1 tsp smoked paprika
- Low-calorie spray oil
- Salt & pepper to season

NUTRITION

- Protein: 35g
- Calories: 450
- Total Fat: 16g
- Saturated Fat: 6g
- Carbohydrates: 40g
- Fibre: 6g
- Sugars: 8g

METHOD

1 In a bowl, mix Dijon mustard, dried thyme, and garlic powder. Rub the mixture onto both sides of the pork chops and season with salt and pepper.

2 Toss the sweet potato wedges and red onion slices with smoked paprika, low-calorie spray oil and a pinch of salt and pepper. Place them in the air fryer and cook at 180°C (350°F) for 10 minutes.

3 After 10 minutes, push the vegetables to the sides and place the pork chops in the centre of the air fryer basket. Cook for 10-12 minutes, flipping halfway through, until the pork chops are golden brown and cooked through.

4 Serve the pork chops with the roasted sweet potatoes and onions on the side.

HERBED LAMB STEAKS

Serves 4

INGREDIENTS

- 4 lamb leg steaks (about 180g each)
- 2 tbsp olive oil
- 1 tbsp lemon juice
- 1 tsp dried rosemary
- 1 tsp dried oregano
- 1 red onion, sliced
- 1 red pepper, sliced
- 200g cherry tomatoes, halved
- 250g pre-cooked couscous
- 2 tbsp chopped fresh parsley
- Low-calorie spray oil
- Salt & pepper to season

NUTRITION

- Protein: 39g
- Calories: 500
- Total Fat: 22g
- Saturated Fat: 8g
- Carbohydrates: 35g
- Fibre: 5g
- Sugars: 7g

METHOD

1 In a bowl, mix olive oil, lemon juice, rosemary, and oregano. Coat the lamb steaks with the mixture and season with salt and pepper.

2 Toss the red onion, red pepper, and cherry tomatoes with low-calorie spray oil and season with salt and pepper. Place them in the air fryer and cook at 180°C (350°F) for 7 minutes.

3 Add the lamb steaks to the air fryer with the vegetables and cook for 10-12 minutes, turning halfway, until the lamb is cooked to your liking.

4 Serve the lamb steaks over the couscous, garnished with chopped parsley and the roasted vegetables.

PEPPERED STEAKS WITH GREEN BEANS

Serves 4

INGREDIENTS

- 4 beef steaks (about 180g each)
- 2 tsp cracked black pepper
- 1 tsp garlic powder
- 300g green beans, trimmed
- 1 red onion, sliced
- 1 tbsp olive oil
- 1 tbsp balsamic vinegar
- Low-calorie spray oil
- Salt to taste

NUTRITION

- Protein: 40g
- Calories: 520
- Total Fat: 24g
- Saturated Fat: 9g
- Carbohydrates: 35g
- Fibre: 7g
- Sugars: 5g

METHOD

1 Rub the beef steaks with cracked black pepper, garlic powder, and salt. Set aside.

2 Toss the green beans and red onion slices with olive oil and balsamic vinegar. Place them in the air fryer and cook at 180°C (350°F) for 7 minutes.

3 Add the steaks to the air fryer, moving the vegetables to the side. Cook for 6-8 minutes, flipping halfway through, until the steaks are cooked to your preference.

4 Serve the steaks with the garlic green beans.

STUFFED PORK TENDERLOIN

Serves 4

INGREDIENTS

- 800g pork tenderloin, butterflied
- 100g chorizo, diced
- 1 red pepper, diced
- 1 tsp smoked paprika
- 200g pre-cooked brown rice
- 1 onion, chopped
- 1 tsp garlic powder
- 2 tbsp chopped fresh flat leaf parsley
- Low-calorie spray oil
- Salt & pepper to season

NUTRITION

- Protein: 36g
- Calories: 450
- Total Fat: 18g
- Saturated Fat: 7g
- Carbohydrates: 35g
- Fibre: 5g
- Sugars: 6g

METHOD

1 Lay the butterflied pork tenderloin flat and sprinkle with smoked paprika, garlic powder, salt, and pepper. Place diced chorizo and red pepper in the centre, then roll up the tenderloin and secure with toothpicks or kitchen twine.

2 Place the tenderloin in the air fryer and cook at 180°C (350°F) for 20-25 minutes, turning halfway through, until cooked through.

3 While the pork is cooking, toss the cooked brown rice with chopped onion, parsley, and a little low-calorie spray oil. Warm in the air fryer for 5 minutes.

4 Slice the stuffed pork tenderloin and serve over the rice.

ROSEMARY LAMB SKEWERS

Serves 4

INGREDIENTS

- 600g lamb fillet, cut into 2cm cubes
- 2 tbsp olive oil
- 1 tbsp lemon juice
- 1 tsp dried rosemary
- 2 red onions, cut into wedges
- 2 yellow peppers, cut into chunks
- 2 courgettes, sliced into thick rounds
- 4 whole-wheat pitta breads
- 4 tbsp low-fat tzatziki sauce
- Low-calorie spray oil
- Salt & pepper to season
- 4 air-fryer safe skewers

METHOD

1 In a bowl, mix olive oil, lemon juice, rosemary, salt, and pepper. Add the lamb cubes and marinate for at least 1 hour.

2 Thread the lamb, onion wedges, pepper chunks and courgette rounds onto skewers. Place in the air fryer and cook at 180°C (350°F) for 15-20 minutes, turning halfway through.

3 Warm the pitta breads in the air fryer for 2 minutes.

4 Serve the lamb skewers with the grilled vegetables in pitta bread, topped with tzatziki sauce.

NUTRITION

- Protein: 38g
- Calories: 520
- Total Fat: 22g
- Saturated Fat: 8g
- Carbohydrates: 45g
- Fibre: 7g
- Sugars: 6g

SPICED BEEF & SWEET POTATO HASH

Serves 4

INGREDIENTS

- 400g lean beef mince
- 2 tsp ground cumin
- 1 tsp smoked paprika
- 1 red onion, chopped
- 2 garlic cloves, minced
- 2 large sweet potatoes, diced
- 1 red pepper, diced
- 2 tbsp fresh corinder, chopped
- 4 eggs
- Low-calorie spray oil
- Salt & pepper to season

NUTRITION

- Protein: 35g
- Calories: 480
- Total Fat: 22g
- Saturated Fat: 8g
- Carbohydrates: 35g
- Fibre: 6g
- Sugars: 5g

METHOD

1 Toss the diced sweet potatoes with smoked paprika, a pinch of salt and a little spray oil. Cook in the air fryer at 180°C (350°F) for 10 minutes.

2 While the potatoes are cooking, brown the beef mince with cumin, garlic, and red onion in a pan.

3 Add the cooked sweet potatoes and diced red pepper to the pan with the beef. Stir to combine and season with salt and pepper.

4 Transfer the mixture to the air fryer and create four small wells. Crack an egg into each well and cook at 180°C (350°F) for 5-7 minutes until the eggs are set to your liking.

5 Garnish with fresh coriander and serve.

BBQ RIBS WITH COLESLAW

Serves 4

INGREDIENTS

- 1kg beef short ribs
- 4 tbsp BBQ sauce
- 1 tbsp smoked paprika
- 1 tsp garlic powder
- 200g cabbage, finely shredded
- 1 carrot, grated
- 4 tbsp low-fat mayonnaise
- 1 tbsp apple cider vinegar
- Low-calorie spray oil
- Salt & pepper to season

NUTRITION

- Protein: 28g
- Calories: 550
- Total Fat: 35g
- Saturated Fat: 12g
- Carbohydrates: 20g
- Fibre: 4g
- Sugars: 6g

METHOD

1 Rub the beef ribs with smoked paprika, garlic powder, salt, and pepper. Brush with BBQ sauce.

2 Place the ribs in the air fryer and cook at 180°C (350°F) for 25-30 minutes, turning and brushing with more BBQ sauce halfway through.

3 While the ribs cook, prepare the coleslaw by mixing the shredded cabbage, grated carrot, mayonnaise and apple cider vinegar.

4 Season with salt and pepper. Serve the ribs with a side of coleslaw.

SPICY BEEF & BEAN CHILI

Serves 4

INGREDIENTS

- 500g lean beef mince
- 1 onion, chopped
- 2 garlic cloves, crushed
- 1 red pepper, diced
- 1 tin (400g) kidney beans, drained and rinsed
- 1 tin (400g) chopped tomatoes
- 2 tbsp tomato puree
- 1 tbsp chili powder
- 1 tsp ground cumin
- 1 tsp smoked paprika
- 100g low-fat sour cream
- 2 tbsp fresh coriander, chopped
- Low-calorie spray oil
- Salt & pepper to season

NUTRITION

- Protein: 35g
- Calories: 450
- Total Fat: 18g
- Saturated Fat: 6g
- Carbohydrates: 35g
- Fibre: 8g
- Sugars: 6g

METHOD

1 Preheat the air fryer to 180°C (350°F). Lightly spray an air fryer-safe dish with low-calorie spray oil. Add the beef mince, chopped onion and garlic to the dish. Place the dish in the air fryer and cook for 10 minutes, stirring halfway through, until the beef is browned and the onion is softened.

2 Once the beef is cooked, stir in the chili powder, ground cumin, smoked paprika, diced red pepper, kidney beans, chopped tomatoes and tomato puree. Mix well to combine.

3 Return the dish to the air fryer and cook for an additional 15-20 minutes at 180°C (350°F), stirring occasionally, until the chilli thickens and the flavours meld together.

4 Serve the chili in bowls with a dollop of low-fat sour cream and a sprinkle of fresh coriander.

SAVOURY BEEF WITH SWEET BERRIES

Serves 4

INGREDIENTS

- 800g lean beef mince
- 1 small onion, finely chopped
- 1 tsp smoked paprika
- 1 tsp ground cumin
- 200g raspberries
- 200g blueberries
- 2 tbsp honey
- Salt to taste
- Low-calorie spray oil

NUTRITION

- Protein: 33g
- Calories: 400
- Total Fat: 18g
- Saturated Fat: 7g
- Carbohydrates: 25g
- Fibre: 5g
- Sugars: 14g

METHOD

1 Lightly spray an air fryer-safe dish with low-calorie spray oil. Add the finely chopped onion and beef mince. Season with smoked paprika, ground cumin, and a pinch of salt. Mix everything together to combine.

2 Place the dish in the air fryer and cook at 180°C (350°F) for 12-15 minutes, stirring halfway through, until the beef is browned and cooked through.

3 Once the beef is cooked, remove the dish from the air fryer. Let it cool slightly for a minute or two.

4 Top with fresh raspberries, blueberries, honey and salt to serve.

GARLIC SOY BEEF, RICE & GREENS

Serves 4

INGREDIENTS

- 600g beef sirloin, sliced into thin strips
- 300g broccoli florets
- 1 red pepper, sliced
- 50g edamame beans
- 200g pre-cooked brown rice
- 3 tbsp soy sauce
- 2 tsp garlic powder
- 2 tbsp olive oil
- 2 tsp ground ginger
- 2 tsp sesame seeds
- Salt & pepper to season

METHOD

1 In a large bowl, combine the beef strips, soy sauce, garlic powder, ground ginger, and olive oil. Toss well to coat the beef evenly. Add the broccoli florets, sliced red pepper, and edamame beans to the bowl and mix everything together.

2 Transfer the beef, vegetables, and edamame mixture to an air fryer-safe dish. Place the cooked brown rice on top of the beef and vegetables, spreading it out evenly.

3 Place the dish in the air fryer and cook at 180°C (350°F) for 12-15 minutes. Stir the mixture halfway through to ensure even cooking. Continue cooking until the beef is cooked to your liking and the vegetables are tender.

4 Once done, remove the dish from the air fryer. Sprinkle the meal with sesame seeds, season to taste and serve.

NUTRITION

- Protein: 50g
- Calories: 550 kcal
- Total Fat: 22g
- Saturated Fat: 6g
- Carbohydrates: 45g
- Fibre: 8g
- Sugars: 6g

♥ FISH

TUNA & SWEET POTATO BOWLS

Serves 4

INGREDIENTS

- 4 large tuna steaks
- 2 large sweet potatoes, cubed
- 1 red onion, diced
- 1 tsp garlic powder
- 1 tsp smoked paprika
- 2 tbsp olive oil
- 1 avocado, sliced
- 1 tbsp lemon juice
- Salt & pepper, to taste

NUTRITION

- Protein: 42g
- Calories: 480 kcal
- Total Fat: 22g
- Saturated Fat: 3.5g
- Carbohydrates: 34g
- Fibre: 8g
- Sugars: 7g

METHOD

1 In a large bowl, toss the sweet potato cubes and red onion with 1 tbsp olive oil, garlic powder, smoked paprika, salt and pepper.

2 Place the sweet potato mixture in the air fryer basket and cook at 200°C (390°F) for 12-15 minutes, shaking the basket halfway through.

3 Rub the tuna steaks with the remaining olive oil, salt, and pepper. After the sweet potatoes have cooked, push them to one side of the basket and add the tuna steaks. Cook at 180°C (350°F) for 6-10 minutes, depending on your preferred doneness.

4 Once cooked, serve the tuna and sweet potatoes in bowls, topped with sliced avocado and a drizzle of lemon juice.

GARLIC PRAWN & VEGGIE MEDLEY

Serves 4

INGREDIENTS

- 800g large prawns, peeled
- 1 courgette, sliced
- 1 red pepper, sliced
- 1 yellow pepper, sliced
- 200g cherry tomatoes, halved
- 2 tsp garlic powder
- 1 tsp smoked paprika
- 1 tbsp olive oil
- Low-calorie spray oil
- Salt & pepper, to taste

NUTRITION

- Protein: 38g
- Calories: 310 kcal
- Total Fat: 11g
- Saturated Fat: 2g
- Carbohydrates: 12g
- Fibre: 4g
- Sugars: 6g

METHOD

1 In a large bowl, toss the prawns with garlic powder, smoked paprika, olive oil, salt and pepper.

2 Lightly spray the sliced courgette, red bell pepper, yellow bell pepper, and cherry tomatoes with low-calorie spray oil. Place the vegetables in the air fryer basket and cook at 200°C (390°F) for 8 minutes.

3 After 8 minutes, add the seasoned prawns to the basket with the vegetables and cook for an additional 6-8 minutes, shaking the basket halfway through, until the prawns are cooked through and the vegetables are tender.

4 Season and serve.

LEMON COD WITH BABY POTATOES

Serves 4

INGREDIENTS

- 4 large cod fillets
- 1 lemon, zested and juiced
- 1 tsp garlic powder
- 1 tsp dried oregano
- 1 tsp dried thyme
- 1 tbsp olive oil
- 200g baby potatoes, halved
- 200g green beans, trimmed
- 1 red onion, sliced
- Low-calorie spray oil
- Salt & pepper, to taste

NUTRITION

- Protein: 38g
- Calories: 380 kcal
- Total Fat: 12g
- Saturated Fat: 2g
- Carbohydrates: 28g
- Fibre: 6g
- Sugars: 4g

METHOD

1 In a small bowl, mix the olive oil, lemon zest, lemon juice, garlic powder, dried oregano, dried thyme, salt and pepper. Rub this mixture over the cod fillets.

2 Lightly spray the baby potatoes with low-calorie spray oil and season with salt and pepper. Place the potatoes in the air fryer basket and cook at 200°C (390°F) for 10 minutes, shaking the basket halfway through.

3 After 10 minutes, add the green beans and red onion to the basket, lightly spraying with more oil if needed. Push the vegetables to one side of the basket and place the cod fillets on the other side.

4 Cook at 180°C (350°F) for an additional 10-12 minutes, or until the cod is cooked through and flakes easily with a fork, and the vegetables are tender. Season and serve.

CRISPY SESAME TUNA WITH BROCCOLI

Serves 4

INGREDIENTS

- 4 large tuna steaks
- 300g broccoli florets
- 1 tbsp sesame oil
- 1 tbsp soy sauce
- 1 tbsp sesame seeds
- 1 tsp garlic powder
- 1 tsp grated ginger
- Low-calorie spray oil
- Salt & pepper, to taste

NUTRITION

- Protein: 53g
- Calories: 490 kcal
- Total Fat: 22g
- Saturated Fat: 4g
- Carbohydrates: 12g
- Fibre: 5g
- Sugars: 3g

METHOD

1 In a small bowl, mix sesame oil, soy sauce, garlic powder, grated ginger, salt and pepper. Rub this mixture over the tuna steaks.

2 Lightly spray the broccoli florets with low-calorie spray oil and season with salt and pepper.

3 Place the broccoli in the air fryer basket and cook at 200°C (390°F) for 5 minutes.

4 After 5 minutes, push the broccoli to one side and add the marinated tuna steaks. Cook at 180°C (350°F) for 6-10 minutes, depending on your preferred doneness.

5 Sprinkle the cooked tuna steaks with sesame seeds and serve with the roasted broccoli.

PRAWN & ASPARAGUS FRITTATA

Serves 4

INGREDIENTS

- 400g large prawns, peeled
- 8 large eggs
- 200g asparagus, chopped
- 100g cherry tomatoes, halved
- 1 tsp garlic powder
- 1 tsp dried oregano
- 1 tbsp olive oil
- Salt & pepper to season

NUTRITION

- Protein: 34g
- Calories: 330 kcal
- Total Fat: 20g
- Saturated Fat: 5g
- Carbohydrates: 6g
- Fibre: 2g
- Sugars: 3g

METHOD

1 In a large bowl, whisk the eggs with garlic powder, dried oregano, salt, and pepper. Stir in the prawns, asparagus, and cherry tomatoes.

2 Lightly spray an air fryer-safe dish with low-calorie spray oil and pour in the egg mixture.

3 Place the dish in the air fryer and cook at 180°C (350°F) for 12-15 minutes, or until the eggs are set and the top is golden.

4 Season and serve.

PRAWN & CAULIFLOWER RICE BOWLS

Serves 4

INGREDIENTS

- 800g large prawns, peeled
- 1 large cauliflower
- 1 red pepper, diced
- 1 green pepper, diced
- 1 red onion, diced
- 1 tbsp olive oil
- 1 tsp garlic powder
- 1 tsp smoked paprika
- Salt & pepper to season

NUTRITION

- Protein: 38g
- Calories: 300 kcal
- Total Fat: 10g
- Saturated Fat: 1.5g
- Carbohydrates: 12g
- Fibre: 6g
- Sugars: 5g

METHOD

1 Grate the cauliflower to make cauliflower rice (or whizz it in a food processor).

2 In a large bowl, toss the prawns with garlic powder, smoked paprika, salt, and pepper.

3 Lightly spray the cauliflower rice, peppers and red onion with low-calorie spray oil. Place them in an air-fryer safe dish and cook at 200°C (390°F) for 8 minutes.

4 After 8 minutes, add the seasoned prawns and cook for an additional 6-8 minutes, shaking the basket halfway through, until the prawns are cooked through, and the vegetables are tender. Season and serve.

SPICY PRAWNS WITH QUINOA

Serves 4

INGREDIENTS

- 500g large prawns
- 2 peppers, sliced
- 1 red onion, cut into wedges
- 1 courgette, sliced
- 1 tsp chili powder
- 1 tsp garlic powder
- 2 tbsp lime juice
- 1 tbsp olive oil
- 180g pre-cooked quinoa
- Salt & pepper to season
- 2 tbsp freshly chopped coriander

NUTRITION

- Protein: 32g
- Calories: 390 kcal
- Total Fat: 12g
- Saturated Fat: 2g
- Carbohydrates: 40g
- Fibre: 8g
- Sugars: 8g

METHOD

1 In a large bowl, toss the prawns with chili powder, garlic powder, lime juice and olive oil. Add the peppers, sliced red onion, and courgette rounds, and mix well to coat everything evenly.

2 Place the prawn and vegetable mixture in the air fryer basket. Cook at 180°C (350°F) for 8-10 minutes, shaking halfway through, until the prawns are pink and cooked through and the vegetables are tender.

3 Once the prawns and vegetables are cooked, remove them from the air fryer and set them aside. Place the cooked quinoa in an air fryer-safe dish, then place the dish in the air fryer basket. Cook the quinoa at 180°C (350°F) for 3-5 minutes, or until heated through and slightly crispy.

4 Combine the air-fried quinoa with the prawn and vegetable mixture. Season and serve.

♥ VEGGIES

PARMESAN AUBERGINE WITH FRESH TOMATOES

Serves 4

INGREDIENTS

- 2 medium aubergines, sliced into rounds
- 100g breadcrumbs
- 2 tbsp grated Parmesan cheese
- 1 tsp dried basil
- 1 tsp dried oregano
- 1 tsp garlic powder
- 1 tbsp olive oil
- 200g passata
- 120g mozzarella cheese, shredded
- 150g ripe plum tomatoes, diced
- Low-calorie cooking spray

NUTRITION

- Protein: 18g
- Calories: 285 kcal
- Total Fat: 13g
- Saturated Fat: 5g
- Carbohydrates: 30g
- Fibre: 8g
- Sugars: 10g

METHOD

1 In a bowl, mix the breadcrumbs, grated Parmesan, dried basil, oregano, garlic powder and olive oil. Coat the aubergine slices in the breadcrumb mixture.

2 Lightly spray an air fryer safe dish. Place the coated aubergine slices in the prepared dish and cook at 375°F (190°C) for 12-15 minutes, until golden and crispy.

3 Remove the dish from the air fryer and top each aubergine slice with a spoonful of passata and a sprinkle of shredded mozzarella. Place the dish back into the air fryer and cook for an additional 3-5 minutes until the cheese is melted and bubbly.

4 Remove from the air fryer and top each serving with a handful of seasoned diced salad tomatoes.

STUFFED MUSHROOMS

Serves 4

INGREDIENTS

- 12 large portobello mushrooms, stems removed
- 200g ricotta cheese
- 100g fresh spinach, chopped
- 1 clove garlic, crushed
- 1 tbsp olive oil
- Salt and pepper to season
- Low-calorie cooking spray

NUTRITION

- Protein: 17g
- Calories: 260 kcal
- Total Fat: 15g
- Saturated Fat: 6g
- Carbohydrates: 10g
- Fibre: 3g
- Sugars: 4g

METHOD

1 In a bowl, mix the ricotta cheese, chopped spinach, crushed garlic, salt, and pepper.

2 Stuff the portobello mushrooms with the ricotta mixture.

3 Lightly spray the air fryer basket with low-calorie cooking spray. Place the stuffed mushrooms in the basket (you will need to cook these in batches) and cook at 375°F (190°C) for 10-12 minutes, until the mushrooms are tender and the ricotta is golden.

HALLOUMI & VEG SKEWERS

Serves 4

INGREDIENTS

- 200g halloumi cheese, cut into cubes
- 1 red pepper, cut into chunks
- 1 yellow pepper, cut into chunks
- 1 courgette, sliced
- 1 red onion, cut into chunks
- 1 tbsp olive oil
- 1 tsp dried oregano
- Salt and pepper to season
- Wooden skewers, soaked in water for 30 minutes

METHOD

1 Toss the halloumi, peppers, courgette, and onion with olive oil, oregano, salt, and pepper.

2 Thread the vegetables and halloumi onto the soaked skewers.

3 Place the skewers in the air fryer basket and cook at 375°F (190°C) for 12-15 minutes, turning halfway through.

4 Season and serve.

NUTRITION

- Protein: 20g
- Calories: 320 kcal
- Total Fat: 22g
- Saturated Fat: 14g
- Carbohydrates: 10g
- Fibre: 3g
- Sugars: 6g

TOFU STIR-FRY WITH PEANUT SAUCE

Serves 4

INGREDIENTS

- 1 block (400g) extra-firm tofu, pressed and cubed
- 1 red pepper, sliced
- 1 yellow pepper, sliced
- 1 courgette, sliced
- 1 tbsp olive oil
- 1 tbsp soy sauce
- 1 tsp garlic powder
- 60g peanut butter
- 2 tbsp soy sauce
- Juice of 1 lime
- 1 tbsp water

NUTRITION

- Protein: 22g
- Calories: 340 kcal
- Total Fat: 22g
- Saturated Fat: 4g
- Carbohydrates: 18g
- Fibre: 5g
- Sugars: 7g

METHOD

1 Toss the tofu and vegetables with olive oil, soy sauce, and garlic powder.

2 Place them in the air fryer basket and cook at 375°F (190°C) for 15 minutes, shaking the basket halfway through.

3 In a small bowl, mix the peanut butter, soy sauce, lime juice, and water to create the peanut sauce.

4 Divide the tofu and vegetables into four portions and drizzle with the peanut sauce.

CAULIFLOWER STEAKS WITH TZATZIKI

Serves 4

INGREDIENTS

- 1 large cauliflower, sliced into thick "steaks"
- 1 tbsp olive oil
- 1 tsp garlic powder
- 1 tsp smoked paprika
- Salt and pepper to season
- 200g Greek yoghurt
- 1 cucumber, grated and drained
- 2 cloves garlic, minced
- Juice of 1 lemon
- 1 tbsp fresh dill, chopped

METHOD

1 Brush the cauliflower steaks with olive oil, garlic powder, smoked paprika, salt, and pepper.

2 Place the cauliflower steaks in the air fryer basket and cook at 375°F (190°C) for 15-18 minutes, flipping halfway through.

3 In a bowl, mix the Greek yogurt, grated cucumber, minced garlic, lemon juice, and fresh dill to make the tzatziki sauce.

4 Serve the cauliflower steaks with a generous dollop of tzatziki.

NUTRITION

- Protein: 17g
- Calories: 240 kcal
- Total Fat: 10g
- Saturated Fat: 3g
- Carbohydrates: 22g
- Fibre: 8g
- Sugars: 8g

STUFFED PINE NUT COURGETTES

Serves 4

INGREDIENTS

- 4 medium courgettes, halved and scooped out
- 200g ricotta cheese
- 50g pine nuts, toasted
- 1 clove garlic, minced
- 1 tbsp olive oil
- Salt and pepper to season
- Low-calorie cooking spray

NUTRITION

- Protein: 15g
- Calories: 280 kcal
- Total Fat: 18g
- Saturated Fat: 7g
- Carbohydrates: 12g
- Fibre: 3g
- Sugars: 5g

METHOD

1 In a bowl, mix the ricotta cheese, toasted pine nuts, minced garlic, salt and pepper. Stuff the courgette halves with the ricotta mixture.

2 Lightly spray the air fryer basket with low-calorie cooking spray. Place the stuffed courgettes in the basket and cook at 375°F (190°C) for 12-15 minutes, until the courgettes are tender and the ricotta is golden.

3 Season and serve.

SQUASH WITH GOAT CHEESE

Serves 4

INGREDIENTS

- 1 medium butternut squash, peeled & diced
- 1 tin (400g) lentils, drained & rinsed
- 1 tbsp olive oil
- 1 tsp ground cumin
- 1 tsp smoked paprika
- Salt and pepper to season
- 120g goat cheese, crumbled

NUTRITION

- Protein: 17g
- Calories: 330 kcal
- Total Fat: 12g
- Saturated Fat: 6g
- Carbohydrates: 42g
- Fibre: 11g
- Sugars: 10g

METHOD

1 Toss the diced butternut squash with olive oil, cumin, smoked paprika, salt and pepper.

2 Place the butternut squash in the air fryer basket and cook at 375°F (190°C) for 15-18 minutes, shaking the basket halfway through.

3 Add the cooked lentils to the air fryer for the last 5 minutes of cooking to heat them through.

4 Divide the butternut squash and lentil mixture into four portions and top each with crumbled goat cheese.

SWEET POTATO & BLACK BEAN TACOS

Serves 4

INGREDIENTS

- 2 large sweet potatoes, diced
- 1 tin (400g) black beans, drained & rinsed
- 1 tbsp olive oil
- 1 tsp ground cumin
- 1 tsp smoked paprika
- ½ tsp chili powder
- Salt and pepper to season
- 240g Greek yoghurt
- 8 small whole wheat tortillas

NUTRITION

- Protein: 18g
- Calories: 350 kcal
- Total Fat: 9g
- Saturated Fat: 2g
- Carbohydrates: 54g
- Fibre: 12g
- Sugars: 9g

METHOD

1 Toss the diced sweet potatoes with olive oil, cumin, smoked paprika, chili powder, salt, and pepper. Place them in the air fryer basket and cook at 375°F (190°C) for 15-18 minutes, shaking the basket halfway through.

2 Warm the tortillas in the air fryer for 2-3 minutes.

3 Divide the sweet potatoes and black beans evenly among the tortillas.

4 Top each taco with Greek yoghurt and serve.

TAHINI CAULIFLOWER BOWL

Serves 4

INGREDIENTS

- 1 large head of cauliflower, cut into florets
- 1 tin (400g) chickpeas, drained & rinsed
- 1 tbsp olive oil
- 1 tsp ground turmeric
- 1 tsp ground cumin
- Salt and pepper to season
- 120g tahini
- Juice of 1 lemon
- 2 tbsp water

METHOD

1 Toss the cauliflower florets and chickpeas with olive oil, turmeric, cumin, salt, and pepper. Place them in the air fryer basket and cook at 375°F (190°C) for 15 minutes, shaking the basket halfway through.

2 In a small bowl, mix the tahini, lemon juice, and water until smooth.

3 Divide the cauliflower and chickpea mixture into four bowls and drizzle each bowl with 30g of tahini dressing.

NUTRITION

- Protein: 16g
- Calories: 320 kcal
- Total Fat: 16g
- Saturated Fat: 2g
- Carbohydrates: 34g
- Fibre: 10g
- Sugars: 4g

AUBERGINE LENTIL SALAD

Serves 4

INGREDIENTS

- 2 medium aubergines, diced
- 1 tin (400g) lentils, drained & rinsed
- 1 tbsp olive oil
- 1 tsp garlic powder
- 1 tsp dried oregano
- Salt and pepper to season
- 200g feta cheese, crumbled

NUTRITION

- Protein: 19g
- Calories: 310 kcal
- Total Fat: 14g
- Saturated Fat: 6g
- Carbohydrates: 31g
- Fibre: 12g
- Sugars: 8g

METHOD

1 Toss the diced aubergine with olive oil, garlic powder, oregano, salt, and pepper.

2 Place them in the air fryer basket and cook at 375°F (190°C) for 15 minutes, shaking the basket halfway through.

3 In a large bowl, combine the cooked eggplant with lentils. Divide the mixture into four portions and top each with crumbled feta cheese.

4 Season and serve.

PAPRIKA BRUSSELS SPROUTS

Serves 4

INGREDIENTS

- 400g Brussels sprouts, halved
- 2 medium sweet potatoes, diced
- 1 tbsp olive oil
- 1 tsp smoked paprika
- 1 tsp garlic powder
- Salt and pepper to season
- 240g cottage cheese

NUTRITION

- Protein: 17g
- Calories: 270 kcal
- Total Fat: 8g
- Saturated Fat: 3g
- Carbohydrates: 38g
- Fibre: 9g
- Sugars: 10g

METHOD

1 Toss the Brussels sprouts and sweet potatoes with olive oil, smoked paprika, garlic powder, salt, and pepper.

2 Place them in the air fryer basket and cook at 375°F (190°C) for 20 minutes, shaking the basket halfway through.

3 Divide the cooked vegetables into four portions and top each with cottage cheese.

4 Season and serve.

COURGETTE & LENTIL YOGHURT FRITTERS

Serves 4

INGREDIENTS

- 2 large courgettes, grated
- ½ tin (200g) cooked lentils, drained & rinsed
- 100g breadcrumbs
- 1 small onion, finely chopped
- 2 cloves garlic, crushed
- 1 tbsp olive oil
- 1 tsp dried thyme
- Low-calorie cooking spray
- Salt and pepper to season
- 240g Greek yoghurt
- 150g green salad leaves

NUTRITION

- Protein: 18g
- Calories: 300 kcal
- Total Fat: 10g
- Saturated Fat: 2g
- Carbohydrates: 36g
- Fibre: 8g
- Sugars: 6g

METHOD

1 In a large bowl, mix the grated courgettes, cooked lentils, breadcrumbs, onion, garlic, olive oil, thyme, salt, and pepper until well combined.

2 Form the mixture into 8 small fritters.

3 Lightly spray the air fryer basket with low-calorie cooking spray. Place the cakes in the basket and cook at 375°F (190°C) for 10-12 minutes, flipping halfway through.

4 Top each fritter with Greek yoghurt and serve with green salad.

SPINACH & PEPPERS WITH COTTAGE CHEESE

Serves 4

INGREDIENTS

- 3 red peppers, sliced
- 3 yellow peppers, sliced
- 120g fresh spinach
- 1 tbsp olive oil
- 200g cooked quinoa
- 240g cottage cheese
- Salt and pepper to season
- Low-calorie cooking spray

NUTRITION

- Protein: 19g
- Calories: 280 kcal
- Total Fat: 8g
- Saturated Fat: 3g
- Carbohydrates: 35g
- Fibre: 6g
- Sugars: 4g

METHOD

1 Toss the sliced peppers with olive oil, salt, and pepper. Place them in the air fryer basket and cook for 10 minutes at 375°F (190°C).

2 While the peppers are cooking, lightly spray an oven-safe dish with oil. After the 10 minutes, transfer the peppers into this dish. Add the cooked quinoa to the dish with the peppers, stirring to combine.

3 Place the dish back into the air fryer and cook for an additional 5 minutes. Add the fresh spinach on top of the quinoa-pepper mixture and cook for another 3-4 minutes, or until the spinach is wilted and everything is heated through.

4 Carefully remove the dish from the air fryer and divide the contents into four portions.

5 Top each serving with 60g of cottage cheese.

EDAMAME STIR-FRY

Serves 4

INGREDIENTS

- 200g edamame beans
- 200g cooked brown rice
- 1 red pepper, sliced
- 1 carrot, julienned
- 1 small onion, sliced
- 2 cloves garlic, minced
- 1 tbsp olive oil
- 2 tbsp soy sauce
- 1 tbsp ginger, grated
- 1 tbsp rice vinegar
- 1 tsp sesame oil
- 1 tbsp sesame seeds
- Salt and pepper to season

NUTRITION

- Protein: 18g
- Calories: 340 kcal
- Total Fat: 12g
- Saturated Fat: 2g
- Carbohydrates: 44g
- Fibre: 8g
- Sugars: 6g

METHOD

1 Toss the edamame with the olive oil and seasoning. Place the edamame in the air fryer basket and cook at 375°F (190°C) for 8-10 minutes, shaking the basket halfway through.

2 In a small bowl, mix the soy sauce, grated ginger, rice vinegar, and sesame oil to make the sauce. After the edamame is done, set it aside.

3 Toss the cooked brown rice, sliced bell pepper, julienned carrot, onion, and garlic with the remaining olive oil, salt, and pepper. Place the mixture in an air fryer-safe dish and cook at 375°F (190°C) for 10-12 minutes, stirring halfway through, until the vegetables are tender.

4 Add the cooked edamame to the rice and vegetable mixture, drizzle with the soy-ginger sauce, and stir to combine. Sprinkle with sesame seeds and serve immediately.

EDAMAME & RICE BALLS

Serves 4

INGREDIENTS

- 200g edamame beans
- 200g cooked jasmine rice
- 100g breadcrumbs
- 1 small onion, finely chopped
- 2 cloves garlic, crushed
- 1 tbsp soy sauce
- 1 tbsp olive oil
- 1 tsp ground cumin
- 1 tsp smoked paprika
- Salt and pepper to season
- Low-calorie cooking spray
- 100g mayonnaise
- 1-2 tbsp sriracha sauce (to taste)

NUTRITION

- Protein: 17g
- Calories: 360 kcal
- Total Fat: 16g
- Saturated Fat: 2g
- Carbohydrates: 44g
- Fibre: 7g
- Sugars: 4g

METHOD

1 Place the edamame in the air fryer basket and cook at 375°F (190°C) for 8-10 minutes, shaking the basket halfway through.

2 In a large bowl, mash the air-fried edamame and mix with the cooked jasmine rice, breadcrumbs, chopped onion, minced garlic, soy sauce, olive oil, cumin, smoked paprika, salt and pepper until well combined.

3 Form the mixture into 12-14 small balls. Lightly spray the air fryer basket with low-calorie cooking spray. Place the rice balls in the basket and cook at 375°F (190°C) for 10-12 minutes, turning halfway through, until golden and crispy.

4 While the rice balls are cooking, mix the mayonnaise and sriracha sauce in a small bowl to create the sriracha mayo dip. Serve the edamame and rice balls with sriracha mayo on the side.

EGGS, EGGS, EGGS

SPINACH & FETA EGG CUPS

Serves 4

INGREDIENTS

- 2 large eggs
- 50g spinach, chopped
- 30g low-fat feta cheese, crumbled
- Salt & pepper to season
- Low-calorie spray oil

NUTRITION

- Protein: 20g
- Calories: 240 kcal
- Total Fat: 16g
- Saturated Fat: 8g
- Carbohydrates: 6g
- Fibre: 2g
- Sugars: 2g

METHOD

1 Whisk the eggs in a bowl and season with salt and pepper.

2 Lightly spray a ramekin or air fryer-safe dish with low-calorie spray oil. Add the spinach and feta cheese, then pour the whisked eggs over the top.

3 Air fry at 180°C (350°F) for 10-12 minutes, or until the eggs are set.

CHEESY EGG-STUFFED PEPPER

Serves 4

INGREDIENTS

- 1 large pepper, halved and deseeded
- 2 large eggs
- 30g grated low-fat cheddar cheese
- Salt & pepper to season
- Low-calorie spray oil

NUTRITION

- Protein: 20g
- Calories: 250 kcal
- Total Fat: 19g
- Saturated Fat: 9g
- Carbohydrates: 2g
- Fibre: 0g
- Sugars: 1g

METHOD

1 Lightly spray the pepper halves with low-calorie spray oil and place them in an air fryer-safe dish.

2 Crack an egg into each bell pepper half, season with salt and pepper, and sprinkle with cheddar cheese.

3 Air fry at 180°C (350°F) for 12-15 minutes, or until the eggs are cooked to your liking.

MUSHROOM & HAM OMELETTE

Serves 4

INGREDIENTS

- 3 large eggs
- 50g mushrooms, sliced
- 50g lean ham, chopped
- Salt & pepper to season
- Low-calorie spray oil

NUTRITION

- Protein: 32g
- Calories: 380 kcal
- Total Fat: 26g
- Saturated Fat: 9g
- Carbohydrates: 7g
- Fibre: 1g
- Sugars: 4g

METHOD

1 Lightly spray an air fryer-safe dish with low-calorie spray oil. Add the mushrooms and ham.

2 Whisk the eggs, season with salt and pepper, and pour over the mushrooms and ham.

3 Air fry at 180°C (350°F) for 10-12 minutes, or until the omelette is set.

BAKED AVOCADO EGG

Serves 4

INGREDIENTS

- 1 avocado, halved and pitted
- 2 large eggs
- 30g low-fat crumbled feta
- Salt & pepper to season
- Low-calorie spray oil

NUTRITION

- Protein: 19g
- Calories: 380 kcal
- Total Fat: 31g
- Saturated Fat: 10g
- Carbohydrates: 11g
- Fibre: 7g
- Sugars: 2g

METHOD

1 Scoop out a bit of the avocado flesh to create space for the eggs.

2 Place the avocado halves in an air fryer-safe dish and crack an egg into each half. Season with salt and pepper, and top with cheese.

3 Air fry at 180°C (350°F) for 10-12 minutes, or until the eggs are cooked to your preference.

EGG & CHICKEN SAUSAGE SCRAMBLE

Serves 4

INGREDIENTS

- 2 large eggs
- 50g cooked chicken sausage, sliced
- 30g grated low-fat mozzarella cheese
- Salt & pepper to season
- Low-calorie spray oil

NUTRITION

- Protein: 30g
- Calories: 400 kcal
- Total Fat: 29g
- Saturated Fat: 12g
- Carbohydrates: 3g
- Fibre: 0g
- Sugars: 2g

METHOD

1 Lightly spray an air fryer-safe dish with low-calorie spray oil. Add the sliced chicken sausage.

2 Whisk the eggs, season with salt and pepper, and pour over the sausage. Sprinkle with mozzarella cheese.

3 Air fry at 180°C (350°F) for 8-10 minutes, or until the eggs are set and the cheese is melted.

EGG & QUINOA BREAKFAST BOWL

Serves 4

INGREDIENTS

- 2 large eggs
- 50g cooked quinoa
- 30g baby spinach, chopped
- Salt & pepper to season
- Low-calorie spray oil

NUTRITION

- Protein: 20g
- Calories: 290 kcal
- Total Fat: 12g
- Saturated Fat: 4g
- Carbohydrates: 26g
- Fibre: 5g
- Sugars: 2g

METHOD

1 Lightly spray an air fryer-safe dish with low-calorie spray oil. Add the cooked quinoa and chopped spinach.

2 Whisk the eggs, season with salt and pepper, and pour over the quinoa and spinach.

3 Air fry at 180°C (350°F) for 10-12 minutes, or until the eggs are set.

EGG-STUFFED PORTOBELLO MUSHROOMS

Serves 4

INGREDIENTS

- 2 large eggs
- 2 large portobello mushrooms, stems removed
- 30g grated Parmesan cheese
- Salt & pepper to season
- Low-calorie spray oil

NUTRITION

- Protein: 26g
- Calories: 300 kcal
- Total Fat: 18g
- Saturated Fat: 8g
- Carbohydrates: 11g
- Fibre: 3g
- Sugars: 5g

METHOD

1 Lightly spray the portobello mushrooms with low-calorie spray oil and place them in an air fryer-safe dish.

2 Crack an egg into each mushroom cap, season with salt and pepper, and top with Parmesan cheese.

3 Air fry at 180°C (350°F) for 12-15 minutes, or until the eggs are cooked to your liking.

EGG & SALMON AVOCADO TOAST

Serves 4

INGREDIENTS

- 2 large eggs
- 1 slice whole grain bread
- 50g smoked salmon
- ½ avocado, mashed
- Salt & pepper to season
- Low-calorie spray oil

NUTRITION

- Protein: 23g
- Calories: 440 kcal
- Total Fat: 30g
- Saturated Fat: 6g
- Carbohydrates: 22g
- Fibre: 9g
- Sugars: 3g

METHOD

1 Lightly spray the slice of bread with low-calorie spray oil and air fry at 180°C (350°F) for 3-5 minutes until toasted.

2 Top the toasted bread with mashed avocado and smoked salmon and put to one side.

3 In an air fryer-safe dish, crack the eggs and air fry at 180°C (350°F) for 6-8 minutes, or until cooked to your liking. Place the eggs on top of the salmon and avocado toast.

EGG & TURKEY RASHERS

Serves 4

INGREDIENTS

- 2 large eggs
- 2 slices turkey rashers
- 30g grated low-fat cheddar cheese
- Salt & pepper to season
- Low-calorie spray oil

NUTRITION

- Protein: 24g
- Calories: 280
- Total Fat: 20g
- Saturated Fat: 7g
- Carbs: 3g
- Fibre: 0g
- Sugars: 1g

METHOD

1 Place the turkey rashers in an air fryer-safe dish and air fry at 180°C (350°F) for 5 minutes.

2 Add the eggs directly to the dish, season with salt and pepper, and sprinkle with cheddar cheese.

3 Continue air frying for another 8-10 minutes, or until the eggs are cooked and the cheese is melted.

COURGETTE & EGG FRITTATA

Serves 4

INGREDIENTS

- 2 large eggs
- 100g courgette, grated
- 30g low-fat feta cheese, crumbled
- Salt & pepper to season
- Low-calorie spray oil

NUTRITION

- Protein: 22g
- Calories: 240
- Total Fat: 17g
- Saturated Fat: 7g
- Carbs: 4g
- Fibre: 1g
- Sugars: 2g

METHOD

1 Lightly spray an air fryer-safe dish with low-calorie spray oil. Add the grated courgette.

2 Whisk the eggs, season with salt and pepper, and pour over the courgette. Top with feta cheese.

3 Air fry at 180°C (350°F) for 10-12 minutes, or until the frittata is set.

EGGS IN PURGATORY

Serves 4

INGREDIENTS

- 2 large eggs
- 100g passata
- 1 garlic clove, crushed
- 1 tsp olive oil
- 1 tsp chilli flakes
- Salt & pepper to season
- Fresh basil leaves (optional)

NUTRITION

- Protein: 16g
- Calories: 180
- Total Fat: 11g
- Saturated Fat: 3g
- Carbs: 8g
- Fibre: 2g
- Sugars: 5g

METHOD

1 Heat the olive oil in an air fryer-safe dish and sauté the garlic until fragrant.

2 Pour in the passata and stir in the chilli flakes. Make two wells in the sauce and crack an egg into each well.

3 Air fry at 180°C (350°F) for 10-12 minutes, or until the eggs are set. Garnish with fresh basil if desired.

SMOKED SALMON & EGG BOWL

Serves 4

INGREDIENTS

- 2 large eggs
- 50g smoked salmon
- 30g baby spinach, chopped
- Salt & pepper to season
- Low-calorie spray oil

NUTRITION

- Protein: 23g
- Calories: 250
- Total Fat: 15g
- Saturated Fat: 4g
- Carbs: 2g
- Fibre: 1g
- Sugars: 1g

METHOD

1 Lightly spray an air fryer-safe dish with low-calorie spray oil and add the chopped spinach.

2 Crack the eggs over the spinach and season with salt and pepper. Lay the smoked salmon over the eggs.

3 Air fry at 180°C (350°F) for 8-10 minutes, or until the eggs are cooked to your preference.

EGGS & CHEDDAR TOAST

Serves 4

INGREDIENTS

- 2 large eggs
- 1 slice whole grain bread
- 30g grated low-fat cheddar cheese
- Salt & pepper to season
- Low-calorie spray oil

NUTRITION

- Protein: 24g
- Calories: 320
- Total Fat: 16g
- Saturated Fat: 8g
- Carbs: 22g
- Fibre: 4g
- Sugars: 2g

METHOD

1 Lightly spray a slice of bread with low-calorie spray oil and place in an air fryer-safe dish.

2 Crack the eggs directly onto the bread, season with salt and pepper, and sprinkle with cheddar cheese.

3 Air fry at 180°C (350°F) for 10-12 minutes, or until the eggs are set and the cheese is melted.

MEDITERRANEAN EGG CUPS

Serves 4

INGREDIENTS

- 2 large eggs
- 30g cherry tomatoes, halved
- 15g black olives, sliced
- 15g low-fat feta cheese, crumbled
- Salt & pepper to season
- Low-calorie spray oil

NUTRITION

- Protein: 21g
- Calories: 230
- Total Fat: 15g
- Saturated Fat: 6g
- Carbs: 4g
- Fibre: 1g
- Sugars: 2g

METHOD

1 Lightly spray a ramekin or air fryer-safe dish with low-calorie spray oil. Add the cherry tomatoes and olives.

2 Crack the eggs into the dish, season with salt and pepper, and top with feta cheese.

3 Air fry at 180°C (350°F) for 10-12 minutes, or until the eggs are cooked to your liking.

MUSHROOM & EGG BREAKFAST SKILLET

Serves 4

INGREDIENTS

- 2 large eggs
- 50g mushrooms, sliced
- 30g grated Parmesan cheese
- Salt & pepper to season
- Low-calorie spray oil

NUTRITION

- Protein: 23g
- Calories: 260
- Total Fat: 18g
- Saturated Fat: 7g
- Carbs: 4g
- Fibre: 1g
- Sugars: 2g

METHOD

1 Lightly spray an air fryer-safe dish with low-calorie spray oil. Add the sliced mushrooms and Parmesan cheese.

2 Crack the eggs over the mushrooms, season with salt and pepper.

3 Air fry at 180°C (350°F) for 10-12 minutes, or until the eggs are set.

SPINACH & EGG STUFFED TOMATOES

Serves 4

INGREDIENTS

- 2 large beef tomatoes, tops sliced off and insides scooped out
- 2 large eggs
- 30g baby spinach, chopped
- 15g grated low-fat mozzarella cheese
- Salt & pepper to season
- Low-calorie spray oil

NUTRITION

- Protein: 22g
- Calories: 230
- Total Fat: 14g
- Saturated Fat: 6g
- Carbs: 6g
- Fibre: 2g
- Sugars: 4g

METHOD

1 Lightly spray the inside of the tomatoes with low-calorie spray oil and place in an air fryer-safe dish.

2 Fill the tomatoes with chopped spinach and crack an egg into each. Top with mozzarella cheese and season with salt and pepper.

3 Air fry at 180°C (350°F) for 10-12 minutes, or until the eggs are cooked to your preference.

EGG-STUFFED SWEET POTATO

Serves 4

INGREDIENTS

- 1 medium sweet potato, baked and halved
- 2 large eggs
- 30g crumbled low-fat feta cheese
- Salt & pepper to season
- Low-calorie spray oil

NUTRITION

- Protein: 21g
- Calories: 310
- Total Fat: 14g
- Saturated Fat: 6g
- Carbs: 31g
- Fibre: 5g
- Sugars: 8g

METHOD

1 Scoop out some of the baked sweet potato flesh to create room for the eggs.

2 Place the sweet potato halves in an air fryer-safe dish. Crack an egg into each half, season with salt and pepper, and top with crumbled feta.

3 Air fry at 180°C (350°F) for 12-15 minutes, or until the eggs are cooked to your liking.

EGG & VEGGIE HASH

Serves 4

INGREDIENTS

- 2 large eggs
- 1 red pepper, diced
- 50g courgette, diced
- ½ red onion, diced
- Salt & pepper to season
- Low-calorie spray oil

NUTRITION

- Protein: 21g
- Calories: 240
- Total Fat: 14g
- Saturated Fat: 4g
- Carbs: 10g
- Fibre: 3g
- Sugars: 5g

METHOD

1 Lightly spray an air fryer-safe dish with low-calorie spray oil. Add the diced bell peppers, courgette, and red onion.

2 Crack the eggs over the veggies, season with salt and pepper.

3 Air fry at 180°C (350°F) for 10-12 minutes, or until the eggs are set and the veggies are tender.

HERBED EGG WHITE BITES

Serves 4

INGREDIENTS

- 4 large egg whites
- 50g low-fat ricotta cheese
- 1 tbsp chopped fresh herbs (parsley, chives, or basil)
- Salt & pepper to season
- Low-calorie spray oil

NUTRITION

- Protein: 21g
- Calories: 140
- Total Fat: 6g
- Saturated Fat: 3g
- Carbs: 3g
- Fibre: 0g
- Sugars: 2g

METHOD

1 Whisk the egg whites in a bowl until frothy. Stir in the ricotta cheese, chopped herbs, salt, and pepper.

2 Lightly spray a silicone muffin mould or air fryer-safe dish with low-calorie spray oil and pour the mixture into the mould.

3 Air fry at 160°C (320°F) for 8-10 minutes, or until the egg white bites are set and slightly golden on top.

TURKISH EGGS

Serves 4

INGREDIENTS

- 2 large eggs
- 150g low-fat Greek yoghurt
- 1 garlic clove, crushed
- 1 tsp olive oil
- 1 tsp butter
- 1 tsp paprika
- Salt & pepper to season

NUTRITION

- Protein: 24g
- Calories: 270 kcal
- Total Fat: 16g
- Saturated Fat: 6g
- Carbs: 6g
- Fibre: 0g
- Sugars: 4g

METHOD

1 Mix the low-fat Greek yogurt with garlic, salt, and pepper in a small bowl. Spread the yoghurt mixture evenly in an air fryer-safe dish. Crack the eggs over the yogurt mixture, keeping them separate. Season with a pinch of salt and pepper and air fry at 180°C (350°F) for 8-10 minutes, or until the eggs are cooked to your preference.

2 While the eggs are cooking, melt the butter in a small pan over medium heat. Add the olive oil and paprika, stirring until the butter turns red.

3 Remove from heat and drizzle the spicy butter sauce over the eggs.

HONEY FETA EGGS

Serves 4

INGREDIENTS

- 2 large eggs
- 50g feta cheese, crumbled
- 1 tbsp honey
- Pinch crushed chili flakes
- 1 roasted red pepper, sliced (jarred is fine)
- 1 tbsp olive oil
- Salt & pepper to season
- 1 tbsp Greek yoghurt

NUTRITION

- Protein: 22g
- Calories: 330 kcal
- Total Fat: 23g
- Saturated Fat: 8g
- Carbohydrates: 11g
- Fibre: 2g
- Sugars: 8g

METHOD

1 Lightly grease an air fryer-safe dish with olive oil. Spread the sliced roasted red pepper evenly across the bottom of the dish.

2 Crack the eggs into the dish, keeping the yolks intact. Season with salt and pepper.

3 Sprinkle the crumbled feta cheese evenly over the eggs. Drizzle the honey over the top, then sprinkle with chili flakes.

4 Place the dish in the air fryer and cook at 180°C (350°F) for 8-10 minutes, or until the eggs are cooked to your desired level of doneness and the feta is slightly melted and golden.

5 Remove the dish from the air fryer and add a spoonful of Greek yogurt on the side for added creaminess. Season and serve.

PROTEIN SNACKS

CRISPY CHICKPEA SNACKS

Serves 1

INGREDIENTS

- 150g canned chickpeas, drained and rinsed
- 1 tsp olive oil
- ½ tsp smoked paprika
- Salt, to taste

NUTRITION
- Protein: 10g
- Calories: 180 kcal
- Total Fat: 6g
- Carbohydrates: 27g
- Fibre: 8g
- Sugars: 2g

METHOD

1 Toss chickpeas with olive oil, smoked paprika, and salt.

2 Air fry at 200°C for 15 minutes, shaking halfway through, until golden and crispy.

EDAMAME BITES

Serves 1

INGREDIENTS

- 120g frozen edamame (in pods)
- ½ tsp sesame oil
- Pinch of sea salt

NUTRITION
- Protein: 11g
- Calories: 140 kcal
- Total Fat: 5g
- Carbohydrates: 10g
- Fibre: 4g
- Sugars: 1g

METHOD

1 Toss the edamame with sesame oil and sea salt.

2 Air fry at 190°C for 8-10 minutes until slightly crispy.

TOFU CUBES WITH SOY SAUCE

Serves 1

INGREDIENTS

- 200g firm tofu, cubed (2½ cm)
- 1 tbsp soy sauce
- ½ tsp garlic powder

NUTRITION
- Protein: 12g
- Calories: 160 kcal
- Total Fat: 8g
- Carbohydrates: 5g
- Fibre: 2g
- Sugars: 1g

METHOD

1 Marinate tofu cubes in soy sauce and garlic powder for 5 minutes.

2 Air fry at 180°C for 12-15 minutes until golden and slightly crispy.

LENTIL FALAFEL BALLS

Serves 1

INGREDIENTS

- 100g cooked lentils
- 1 tbsp whole wheat flour
- ¼ tsp cumin
- Salt and pepper, to taste

NUTRITION
- Protein: 10g
- Calories: 100 kcal
- Total Fat: 1g
- Carbohydrates: 15g
- Fibre: 4g
- Sugars: 1g

METHOD

1 Mix lentils, flour, cumin, salt, and pepper. Form into 6-8 small balls.

2 Air fry at 190°C for 10-12 minutes until firm and golden.

ROASTED ALMONDS WITH SPICES

Serves 1

INGREDIENTS

- 40g almonds
- ½ tsp olive oil
- ¼ tsp smoked paprika
- Pinch of salt

NUTRITION
- Protein: 8g
- Calories: 220 kcal
- Total Fat: 18g
- Carbohydrates: 6g
- Fibre: 4g
- Sugars: 1g

METHOD

1 Toss almonds with olive oil, smoked paprika, and salt.

2 Air fry at 160°C for 8-10 minutes, shaking halfway through.

HALLOUMI FINGERS

Serves 1

INGREDIENTS

- 75g halloumi, cut into 4-5 strips
- ½ tsp olive oil
- Oregano, to taste

NUTRITION
- Protein: 11g
- Calories: 160 kcal
- Total Fat: 12g
- Carbohydrates: 2g
- Fibre: 0g
- Sugars: 0g

METHOD

1 Toss halloumi strips with olive oil and oregano.

2 Air fry at 180°C for 6-8 minutes until golden and crispy.

PEANUT BUTTER STUFFED DATES

Serves 1

INGREDIENTS

- 4 medjool dates, pitted
- 1 tbsp peanut butter

NUTRITION
- Protein: 10g
- Calories: 150 kcal
- Total Fat: 8g
- Carbohydrates: 24g
- Fibre: 4g
- Sugars: 20g

METHOD

1 Stuff each date with a small amount of peanut butter.

2 Air fry at 180°C for 3-5 minutes until warm.

CRISPY BROAD BEANS

Serves 1

INGREDIENTS

- 100g tinned broad beans, drained
- 1 tsp olive oil
- ½ tsp chilli powder
- Salt, to taste

NUTRITION
- Protein: 10g
- Calories: 140 kcal
- Total Fat: 4g
- Carbohydrates: 16g
- Fibre: 5g
- Sugars: 1g

METHOD

1 Toss broad beans with olive oil, chilli powder, and salt.

2 Air fry at 200°C for 12-15 minutes until crispy.

PARMESAN COURGETTE CHIPS

Serves 1

INGREDIENTS

- 1 medium courgette
- 10g grated Parmesan cheese
- Salt and pepper, to taste

NUTRITION
- Protein: 10g
- Calories: 70 kcal
- Total Fat: 3g
- Carbohydrates: 4g
- Fibre: 1g
- Sugars: 1g

METHOD

1 Slice the courgette into 10-12 slices and sprinkle with Parmesan, salt, and pepper.

2 Air fry at 180°C for 8-10 minutes until crispy.

BLACK BEAN QUESADILLA SLICES

Serves 1

INGREDIENTS

- 1 small whole wheat tortilla
- 50g black beans, mashed
- 15g low-fat cheddar cheese

NUTRITION
- Protein: 11g
- Calories: 160 kcal
- Total Fat: 5g
- Carbohydrates: 20g
- Fibre: 4g
- Sugars: 1g

METHOD

1 Spread black beans and cheese on half of the tortilla.

2 Fold and air fry at 180°C for 5-6 minutes until golden. Cut into slices and serve.

SPICED CASHEW MIX

Serves 1

INGREDIENTS

- 30g cashew nuts
- 60g canned chickpeas, drained and rinsed
- ½ tsp olive oil
- ¼ tsp curry powder

NUTRITION
- Protein: 10g
- Calories: 210 kcal
- Total Fat: 12g
- Carbohydrates: 18g
- Fibre: 4g
- Sugars: 2g

METHOD

1 Toss cashew nuts and chickpeas with olive oil and curry powder.

2 Air fry at 160°C for 10-12 minutes, shaking halfway through, until the cashews are toasted and the chickpeas are crispy.

TEMPEH CUBES WITH SOY GLAZE

Serves 1

INGREDIENTS

- 100g tempeh, cubed (2½ cm)
- 1 tbsp soy sauce
- ½ tsp maple syrup

NUTRITION
- Protein: 11g
- Calories: 150 kcal
- Total Fat: 6g
- Carbohydrates: 10g
- Fibre: 2g
- Sugars: 3g

METHOD

1 Toss tempeh cubes in soy sauce and maple syrup.

2 Air fry at 180°C for 12-15 minutes until caramelised.

KALE CHIPS

Serves 1

INGREDIENTS

- 50g kale leaves
- 10g nutritional yeast
- Low-calorie spray oil

NUTRITION
- Protein: 10g
- Calories: 60 kcal
- Total Fat: 1.5g
- Carbohydrates: 7g
- Fibre: 3g
- Sugars: 0g

METHOD

1 Toss kale with nutritional yeast and spray oil.

2 Air fry at 170°C for 5-7 minutes until crispy.

CAULIFLOWER BITES WITH ALMOND CRUST

Serves 1

INGREDIENTS

- 100g cauliflower florets
- 2 tsp olive oil
- 30g ground almonds
- 15g grated Parmesan cheese
- ½ tsp garlic powder

NUTRITION
- Protein: 10g
- Calories: 200 kcal
- Total Fat: 14g
- Carbohydrates: 11g
- Fibre: 5g
- Sugars: 2g

METHOD

1 Toss the cauliflower florets in olive oil until they are lightly coated. In a separate bowl, mix the ground almonds, Parmesan cheese, garlic powder, salt, and pepper. Coat the oiled cauliflower florets in the almond mixture until well-covered.

2 Air fry at 180°C for 10-12 minutes until crispy and golden.

SWEET POTATO & LENTIL BALLS

Serves 1

INGREDIENTS

- 100g raw sweet potato, grated
- 50g cooked lentils
- ½ tsp cumin
- 1 tbsp whole wheat flour or 1 egg (for binding)
- Salt and pepper, to taste

NUTRITION
- Protein: 10g
- Calories: 130 kcal
- Total Fat: 1.5g
- Carbohydrates: 22g
- Fibre: 6g
- Sugars: 4g

METHOD

1 Mix the raw grated sweet potato, cooked lentils, cumin, flour or egg, salt, and pepper together in a bowl until well combined. Form the mixture into 6-8 small balls.

2 Air fry at 180°C for 12-15 minutes, shaking halfway through, until the balls are golden and the sweet potato is tender.

SPICY PUMPKIN SEEDS

Serves 1

INGREDIENTS

- 40g pumpkin seeds
- ½ tsp chilli powder
- Low-calorie spray oil

NUTRITION
- Protein: 10g
- Calories: 140 kcal
- Total Fat: 10g
- Carbohydrates: 4g
- Fibre: 2g
- Sugars: 0g

METHOD

1 Toss pumpkin seeds with chilli powder and spray oil.

2 Air fry at 160°C for 5-7 minutes until toasted.

PEA FRITTERS

Serves 1

INGREDIENTS

- 100g frozen peas, thawed
- 1 egg
- 1 tbsp whole wheat flour

NUTRITION
- Protein: 11g
- Calories: 110 kcal
- Total Fat: 3g
- Carbohydrates: 14g
- Fibre: 3g
- Sugars: 2g

METHOD

1 Blend the peas, egg, and flour until coarsely combined. Form into 4-6 small fritters.

2 Air fry at 190°C for 10-12 minutes until set and golden.

PAPRIKA BUTTER BEANS

Serves 1

INGREDIENTS

- 100g canned butter beans, drained
- 1 tsp olive oil
- ½ tsp smoked paprika

NUTRITION
- Protein: 11g
- Calories: 150 kcal
- Total Fat: 4g
- Carbohydrates: 19g
- Fibre: 5g
- Sugars: 2g

METHOD

1 Toss butter beans with olive oil and smoked paprika.

2 Air fry at 200°C for 10-12 minutes until crispy.

ROASTED CARROT & QUINOA BITES

Serves 1

INGREDIENTS

- 100g grated carrot
- 50g cooked quinoa
- 1 egg
- ½ tsp mixed herbs

NUTRITION

- Protein: 10g
- Calories: 110 kcal
- Total Fat: 3g
- Carbohydrates: 15g
- Fibre: 3g
- Sugars: 2g

METHOD

1 Mix the grated carrot, quinoa, egg, and herbs until well combined.

2 Form into 6-8 small bites.

3 Air fry at 180°C for 10-12 minutes until crisp on the edges.

ALMOND BUTTER APPLE SLICES

Serves 1

INGREDIENTS

- 1 apple, sliced (8-10 slices)
- 1 tbsp almond butter

NUTRITION

- Protein: 10g
- Calories: 130 kcal
- Total Fat: 8g
- Carbohydrates: 15g
- Fibre: 3g
- Sugars: 10g

METHOD

1 Spread almond butter evenly on the apple slices.

2 Air fry at 180°C for 5 minutes until warm.